INSIDE OUT

WHY STRONG EOS COMPANIES HAVE WEAK SALES TEAMS

(AND HOW TO REIGNITE GROWTH)

**WALTER CROSBY &
MATTHEW DAVID ANDERSON**

Published by: Helix Sales Development

Milford, MI, USA

Paperback ISBN: 978-1-959911-45-6
Ebook ISBN: 978-1-959911-46-3

Printed in the United States of America

Walter loves hearing from readers. You can reach him at
walter@helixsalesdevelopment.com or https://helixsalesdevelopment.com

TABLE OF CONTENTS

Introduction:
The Silent Crisis in B2B Sales

I f you're running a mid-sized company on the Entrepreneurial Operating System (EOS®), you're living a puzzling paradox. Your internal processes hum smoothly, your teams move in perfect alignment, and you're hitting most of your organizational goals. Yet, when it comes to sales, something feels... off.

You're not alone.

Across industries, B2B sales teams face a silent crisis. Win rates plummet, sales cycles stretch endlessly, and forecasts—once reliable—now feel more like wishful thinking. Perhaps most troubling? The gap between your top performers and the rest of the sales team keeps widening.

Why is this happening? And more importantly, why hasn't your EOS implementation fixed it?

The answer lies in a perfect storm that's fundamentally altered the B2B sales landscape.

Your buyers are drowning in information. They've heard every pitch, seen every feature comparison, and devoured countless customer testimonials before ever speaking to a salesperson. The Fortune 500 now invests more in training buyers than in training sellers. Your prospects arrive armed with sophisticated negotiation tactics, close-deflecting techniques, and battle-tested strategies to extract maximum value.

Meanwhile, ever-more-aggressive sales teams saturate every channel, amplifying a deafening sameness. Everyone blasts the same AI-generated emails, deploys identical chatbots, and follows eerily similar scripts. In these hyper-competitive markets, your groundbreaking feature gets copied within months. Your unique selling point? It's drowning in a chorus of competitors shouting the same thing.

The result? Your buyers swim in a sea of sameness, struggling to tell one option from another.

EOS has given you powerful tools to organize your company internally. But in this new landscape, internal alignment isn't enough. To thrive in today's market, you need a fundamental shift in how you approach sales—a shift that EOS alone can't provide.

What is this shift? How can you implement it today and get a head start on your competitors? This book contains the answers.

But first, we must understand the true nature of our challenge.

Losing Control

You know the scene. The monthly sales review meeting. Your pipeline is full, activity metrics look strong, and every sales stage shows healthy progression. On paper, everything points to a solid quarter ahead.

Yet, in your gut, something feels wrong.

Deals you thought were certain keep stalling. Prospects who seemed engaged suddenly go dark. Worst of all are the deals you lose to competitors you never knew were in the running. Your top performers—the ones who could always be counted on to save the quarter—are struggling. Even with a perfectly implemented EOS system, predictable revenue feels further away than ever.

If this sounds familiar, you're experiencing a fundamental shift that is transforming B2B sales in most industries today—one that most companies haven't begun to understand fully. The balance of power between sales teams and buyers has shifted. Your buyers have seized control, and they're not giving it back.

This isn't just another market cycle or a temporary trend. It's a permanent transformation in how B2B buying decisions are made, exposing a fatal flaw in our approach to sales.

The Illusion of Control

For the last seven decades, what I like to call "the Standard Sales Model" has been built on a simple assumption: the seller guides the buyer through a series of stages toward a purchase decision.

You've seen this model. You've probably built your entire sales operation around it:

- The first meeting to understand the needs

- Demo to showcase solutions

- Proposal to present options

- Negotiation to close the deal

For the past 70 years, this model has been taught in every sales training session, embedded in every CRM, and reinforced by every sales methodology. It's so ubiquitous that we've stopped questioning its core premise: that we, as sellers, control the journey.

But today's buyers aren't following our carefully designed stages. They're not waiting for our discovery questions to understand their needs. They're not relying on our demos to evaluate solutions. And they're certainly not letting us guide them through our sales process.

Instead, they research independently, compare options silently, and often make decisions before engaging with sales. When they do reach out, it's on their terms, not ours. And the carefully crafted sales journey we've designed? They ignore it completely.

False Comfort

How do most companies respond to this loss of control? By doubling down on what they *can* control. More pipeline reviews. More detailed sales stages. More activity metrics. More internal processes. In short, good old-fashioned micro-managing.

EOS gives us powerful tools for this internal control: rocks that define clear sales goals, L10 meetings that drive accountability, and scorecards that measure every aspect of sales performance. These tools create the comforting illusion that we're still in charge of the sales process.

But the devastating truth is the more we focus on controlling our internal sales process, the wider the gap between our metrics and market reality.

Think about your own experience. Your pipeline reviews show healthy deals, but how many of those close? Your activity metrics hit all the targets, but do those activities drive results? Your sales stages show progression, but does that progression reflect real buyer intent?

I recently spoke with a company that exemplified this paradox. Their EOS implementation was textbook perfect. Every sales metric was green. Their L10 meetings ran like clockwork. Their sales team hit every activity goal. Yet their actual results kept declining. Why? Because all their internal excellence meant nothing to buyers who had seized control of the purchasing process.

The Brutal Reality

This shift in control of the sales process isn't subtle. It's transforming every aspect of B2B sales.

Your carefully timed follow-ups? Buyers engage on their schedule, not yours. Your skillfully crafted discovery questions? They've already discovered what they need to know. Your polished sales presentation? They've seen five similar ones before you arrived. Your structured sales process? They're following their own path, not yours.

They arrive armed with research, comparisons, and often a preferred choice before your sales team enters the picture.

The most devastating fact is that your buyers often know more about your market, competitors, and pricing than your salespeople.

The Fortune 500 has flipped the script, investing more resources into training buyers than sellers invest in their own teams. Your prospects don't just appear prepared; they arrive armed with sophisticated negotiation tactics, close-deflecting techniques, and battle-tested strategies to extract maximum value.

The Control Paradox

Paradoxically, everything we do to regain control of our selling process reduces it further. We implement more rigid sales processes, and our buyers become more distant. We ask more discovery questions, and they become more guarded about information. We follow up more persistently, and they retreat further into silence.

The systems we build to create predictability in our sales process make our results less predictable. Our attempts to control the journey push our buyers further away from the path we've designed for them.

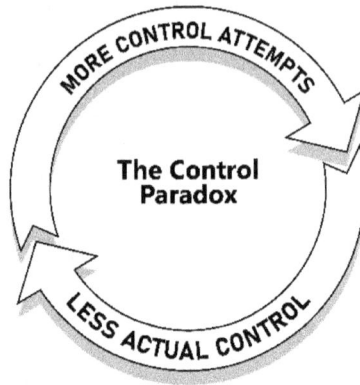

This isn't just frustrating—it's devastating to our ability to grow our companies predictably. You probably recognize the symptoms:

- Your carefully crafted sales messages are brushed aside, lost in the noise of countless similar pitches.

- Your sales team, once confident closers, now struggle even to get a foot in the door.

- Your sales team feels they can't close sales without offering discounts or price breaks to make you cheaper than your competitors. They think that most deals come down to price rather than your superior features and benefits.

- Your forecasts, critical for business planning, become increasingly unreliable.

☐ Your margins erode as buyers cannot distinguish real value and default to price-based decisions.

The Painful Truth

The hardest part? This loss of control isn't temporary. It's not something we can reverse with better training, processes, or execution of EOS. The power shift is permanent, and it's accelerating.

Every new technology, information source, and buying tool gives your buyers more power. The more we try to regain control using traditional sales approaches, the more we push our buyers away.

We cannot forecast revenue when we can't control the sales process. Similarly, we cannot plan hiring, investment, or expansion, and the foundation of strategic business growth crumbles.

But this is just the beginning of our problems. Because while we've been losing control of the sales process, something even more insidious has been happening to our ability to differentiate ourselves in the market. And that's what we need to understand next.

The Sameness Spiral

A sales leader sits in the back of her conference room, watching her top performer deliver their newly refined sales presentation. The story perfectly aligns with the Three Uniques from their V/TO. The value proposition follows every best practice they've learned. The features and benefits that differentiate their marqué product are crystal clear. After months of work with their EOS Implementer, they've finally captured what makes them special.

Then she has a chilling realization: she's heard this exact presentation before. It's not just similar. Aside from some small differences in wording and emphasis, it's practically identical to their competitors' presentations.

How is this possible? They've done everything right. They've followed every step of the EOS model. Their Three Uniques truly are unique to them. Yet somehow, in trying to tell their unique story, they sound just like everyone else.

This isn't an isolated incident. It's the devastating consequence of a system that turns every attempt at differentiation into another proof of sameness.

The Standard Sales Model

The root of this problem goes deeper than most realize. For 70 years, the professional sales industry has perfected the Standard Sales Model. Sales trainers and consultants have documented, systematized, and spread "best practices" across every industry.

The result? A universal playbook that every B2B company follows:

Start with discovery questions: "What keeps you up at night?" "What are your biggest challenges?" "Where do you see your business in three years?" Questions that were once innovative ways to understand customers have become clichés that signal, we're following a script.

Move to value propositions: "We provide innovative solutions..." "Our unique approach..." "What sets us apart..." Phrases that are supposed to differentiate instead confirm we're just like everyone else.

Handle objections with standard responses: "I understand your concern..." "Let me address that..." "What I hear you saying..."

Templates meant to build trust now destroy it by revealing we follow a formula.

Close with ROI calculations and proof points that all look suspiciously similar because we all use the same frameworks to present them.

This standardization promised to make sales success repeatable. Instead, it's made genuine differentiation impossible.

Amplifying the Echo

If the Standard Sales Model created this problem, modern technology has turned it into a crisis, amplifying sameness across every aspect of the sales process.

It starts with our CRM systems. These platforms enforce standardized stages, activities, and workflows in the name of "sales process optimization." Every interaction is categorized, templated, and measured against universal benchmarks. Sales managers celebrate when their teams "follow the process consistently," not realizing that this consistency makes them indistinguishable from their competitors using the same CRM playbooks.

Sales automation tools take this standardization further. They promise personalized outreach at scale but deliver identical messages dressed up in mail-merge fields. Every company uses the same sequencing patterns: the initial touch, the follow-up, the "break-up" email. Even the attempt to sound casual and personal has become formulaic. "Just bumping this to the top of your in-box" appears in thousands of identical follow-ups every day.

AI has accelerated this trend to frightening levels. AI-powered sales tools generate messages that all sound alike because they're trained on the same sales methodologies and "successful" templates. The algorithms designed to help us connect more effectively homogenize sales communication across entire industries.

Social selling, meant to humanize sales, has created new forms of sameness. LinkedIn has become a sea of identical "thought leadership" posts, connection requests, and sales messages. Everyone follows the same "social selling" best practices, creating profiles that look alike, sharing similar content, and engaging in predictable ways. We're all trying to be authentic on the same platforms, using the same techniques, creating a deafening chorus of sameness.

When Unique Becomes Universal

This creates a particularly painful paradox for companies running on EOS. The Three Uniques exercise is supposed to help us capture what differentiates our business. Companies invest significant time with their Implementers, drilling down to what makes them special. They align their entire organization around these differentiators.

This internal focus is a natural consequence of how the Three Uniques are developed. Every EOS process starts inward. Implementers and leaders ask questions like: What are we good at? What do we believe in? What makes us proud of our company?

These are important questions for building a strong culture and aligned team. But they don't address the critical external question: What makes us meaningfully different in ways *our buyers* care about and understand?

However, almost every set of Three Uniques I've seen across dozens of EOS companies reflects the entrepreneur's insider perspective, not what matters to buyers. They capture what the leadership team believes makes them special, not what their market values or perceives.

Even when companies identify genuinely distinctive internal characteristics, something goes wrong when their sales teams try to communicate these carefully crafted uniques. The very act of selling transforms their authentic differences into generic claims that buyers have heard before.

Why? Because they're using the Standard Sales Model to communicate their uniqueness. They're taking what's truly special about their companies and forcing it through a sales process that makes everything sound the same. The more forcefully they assert their uniqueness, the more they sound like their competitors, who all assert their uniqueness with equal vigor.

This creates a compound problem. Not only do their Three Uniques often miss what buyers care about, but the way they communicate these Uniques makes them sound just like everyone else. It's a double trap of internal focus and standardized communication.

The Differentiation Trap

Every attempt to break free from commoditization pushes us deeper into it.

This leads us to the most devastating realization: the harder we try to stand out, the more we sound like everyone else.

Consider how this plays out in practice. When companies realize their standard sales approach isn't working, they try to elevate their game. They move to more "consultative" selling but use the same consultative techniques as their competitors. They emphasize "trusted advisor" status but follow everyone else's trust-building playbook. They focus on "building relationships" but use identical relationship-building approaches.

Each attempt to differentiate follows a predictable pattern: First, it identifies what's missing from the current approach. Then, it adopts the widely taught "best practice" solution. Finally, it sounds exactly like every other company that identified the same gap and adopted the same solution.

Even the Truth Can't Set You Free

Even companies with genuinely unique offerings can't escape this trap.

Let me share a real example that drives this point home. One of my prospective clients had what seemed like a foolproof, unique selling proposition. They were the only company in their multi-state region that could genuinely extend the life of asphalt roads. Unlike competitors who merely apply a top coat to make roads look new, their service replaced the maltenes that the sun leaches from asphalt, extending road life by 20-30%.

On paper, it should have been an easy sale. My prospective client offered a superior solution with tangible, long-term benefits. No one else in their market could match their offering. The cost savings over time were significant, and the environmental benefits of not having to replace roads as frequently were clear. It was innovation at its finest—a true breakthrough in road maintenance technology.

Yet despite these compelling advantages, they struggled to gain traction in the market. Most potential buyers lumped them in with their top-coat competitors. Prospects were highly skeptical that the service worked as claimed. Years of dealing with quick-fix solutions that didn't deliver on their promises had made these buyers cynical and resistant to new pitches, no matter how revolutionary they seemed.

What's more, the uniqueness of their offering sometimes worked against them. Decision-makers in local governments and private-sector companies were often risk-averse, preferring to stick with the familiar, even if it was less effective. The innovative nature of the solution, rather than being a selling point, became a hurdle to overcome.

Their salespeople were fighting an uphill battle at every turn. They had plenty of facts, figures, and compelling case studies, but prospects usually ignored them. The sales cycle dragged on, with multiple stakeholders needing convincing and reams of proof required at every step. Their real differentiation drowned in a sea of sameness created by their sales approach.

The Buyer's Dilemma

From the buyer's perspective, this sameness spiral creates an impossible situation for salespeople. Every day, buyers face multiple vendors, all claiming to be different, all using identical approaches to prove it. They hear similar value propositions, field the same discovery questions, and review comparable ROI calculations. Each company insists on its uniqueness while demonstrating its sameness through every interaction.

This fuels a deepening crisis in B2B sales. The more skeptical buyers become, the harder companies work to prove their differentiation. This increased effort drives them deeper into standardized sales approaches, making them sound more similar. Each turn of this cycle increases buyer skepticism and desperation to stand out, accelerating the spiral.

We're not just facing a sales execution problem. We're trapped in a system that transforms every attempt at differentiation into proof of sameness. Our efforts to stand out prove that we're just like everyone else. Even perfect execution of EOS can't solve this because the problem isn't internal alignment, it's the fundamental breakdown of how B2B sales works.

This is more than a collection of troubling trends. It's evidence that everything we know about B2B sales—everything we've been taught, implemented, and believed—is not just failing. It's actively working against us.

We're not just dealing with a market downturn. We're watching the complete collapse of the system that built our businesses.

The implications are staggering. If we can't sell effectively, we can't grow predictably. We can't plan, invest, or scale. The very foundation of many successful businesses is cracking beneath our feet.

More training won't fix this. Better processes won't solve it. Perfect EOS implementation won't save us. The system is broken, and every attempt to salvage it with traditional solutions only hastens its collapse.

What's needed isn't incremental improvement. It's not better execution of proven methods. Those methods are the problem. What's needed is a fundamental reimagining of how B2B sales works in today's reality.

THE BUYER-FIRST PIVOT™

O ur analysis of B2B sales has revealed a troubling paradox: The better companies master traditional sales approaches, the worse their results become. The more perfectly they execute proven techniques, the less effective they are. The more faithfully they follow established best practices, the faster their performance declines.

This seems impossible. How can better execution of proven methods produce worse outcomes? How can more training, better processes, and stricter adherence to best practices reduce sales effectiveness?

Yet the evidence surrounds us. A global software company invests millions in sales training, only to see win rates drop 20%. A manufacturing firm implements a rigorous new sales process and then watches sales cycles lengthen. A professional services firm rolls out a slick new marketing campaign emphasizing its uniqueness, and while it's getting more attention, buyers seem, if anything, more distant.

Even a perfect implementation of EOS—with its powerful tools for clarity, alignment, and accountability—can't escape this paradox. The better companies execute their internal systems, the wider the gap between their internal excellence and their buyers' reality grows.

This contradiction reveals something profound: We're not just doing something wrong; we're doing the wrong thing entirely. The solution will not be found in better executing existing approaches. It requires fundamentally rethinking our basic assumptions about how B2B sales work.

The Revelation That Changes Everything

I discovered this truth the hard way nearly 20 years ago. I had just taken a new job selling a technical product in a rapidly commoditizing market. Our competitors were Fortune 500 companies with bigger marketing budgets, stronger brands, and well-resourced sales teams. Following the Standard Sales Model, I was getting crushed.

I tried everything: better discovery questions, stronger value propositions, and more compelling ROI calculations. Each improvement made buyers more resistant, not less. My sales training told me to push harder, ask better questions, and present more convincingly. But every "improvement" in my sales approach produced worse results.

In desperation, I stopped thinking about how to sell and started obsessing about how buyers in this new-to-me market made decisions. I studied their process, their concerns, and their internal dynamics. I realized that I might have a chance if I could figure out how to become an asset to their decision-making process rather than an obstacle.

> *It was only when I completely ran out of traditional options that I was forced to confront a terrifying question: What if everything I knew about sales was the problem?*

The results were stunning. In less than a year, this pivot to buyer-centric selling produced record sales—an epiphany that has guided my career ever since.

I learned that B2B sales consultants have been solving the wrong problem. Our efforts to improve sales effectiveness focus on improving our sales process, strengthening our value proposition, and clarifying our differentiation. However, these efforts miss the fundamental shift required.

The solution isn't to improve our ability to push our perspective. Instead, we must start from the buyer's perspective and work backward. Everything we do in sales must be focused on helping our buyers succeed.

This insight explains the paradox we opened with and points to its solution. Better execution of traditional sales approaches fails because it makes us more obviously "salesy" to increasingly skeptical buyers. More rigorous processes create more resistance from buyers who refuse to follow our preferred path. Clearer differentiation messages sound more like the similar claims they've heard from every other vendor.

The Buyer-First Perspective

This experience brings us a crucial insight: Buyers don't want to be sold. They don't trust that a sales process will ever benefit them. But they still have problems, unmet desires, dreams, and aspirations.

You've witnessed this truth yourself. The same procurement officer who stonewalls your sales ef-

While buyers don't like to be sold, they desperately want to succeed—and they will enthusiastically buy solutions they believe will help them succeed.

forts will stand in line for hours to buy the latest iPhone. The CEO who won't return your calls pre-ordered a Tesla Cybertruck years before it existed.

The Buyer's World vs. Seller's World

Buyer First Sales Process

This isn't just consumer behavior. Even in the most commoditized B2B markets, buying happens every day. The difference is that buyers engage enthusiastically when they feel in control of the decision-making process. When they feel they're being manipulated by your sales process, they resist.

The evidence for this principle appears everywhere. Research from Harvard Business School shows that when people feel pushed toward a decision, they experience psychological reactance, an instinctive resistance to perceived manipulation. However, their engagement and commitment increase when they feel in control of their choice.

This explains why traditional sales approaches are failing. Every tactic in the Standard Sales Model is designed to push buyers toward our desired outcome. But modern buyers, armed with information and alternatives, reject this pushing. The harder we push, the more they resist.

Flipping the Model

The traditional approach pushes from the inside out. We start with our sales process, story, and differentiation and try to force buyers to conform to our perspective. Even EOS's Three Uniques typically reflect what we think makes us special rather than what buyers care about.

Consider how this plays out in practice:

□ Our sales process assumes control we don't have

□ Our features-and-benefits claims trigger skepticism we can't overcome

- Our value propositions focus on what we think matters, not what buyers value

The Buyer-First Pivot flips this model entirely. We start from the outside—the buyer's perspective, process, and needs—and work our way in. Instead of pushing our story, we align with their reality.

This simple shift in perspective solves the core problems we identified in previous chapters.

It addresses our loss of control by acknowledging and embracing the buyer's control of the process. Instead of fighting this reality, we align with it.

It breaks the sameness spiral by starting with what buyers care about rather than what we think makes us special. When you truly understand your buyers' perspective, you separate yourself from every other salesperson who is constantly trying to sell to your buyer. Then, you can use what you learn from your buyer to genuinely differentiate your solution.

It bypasses traditional sales' systemic failure by building a new system around buyer reality rather than seller preferences.

The Four Essential Transformations

This pivot requires four fundamental transformations in how we approach B2B sales.

First, we must transform our process. The linear sales stages of the Standard Sales Model assume control we don't have. Instead, we need flexible processes that align with a buyer's decisions. This means rethinking everything from how we measure progress to how we define success in our EOS Scorecard.

Second, our messaging must evolve. Instead of leading with how we're different, we start by acknowledging what buyers already believe about our category. This counter-intuitive approach builds credibility and opens the door for real differentiation based on what matters to buyers, not just what we think makes us special.

Third, we need a new type of salesperson. The smooth-talking closer who could "sell ice to Eskimos" is obsolete. We need buying guides who can understand complex decision processes, build trust through transparency, and help prospects make confident choices—even if that choice is not to buy from us.

Finally, sales leadership must transform. Pipeline reviews and activity metrics don't drive buyer success. We need leaders who can coach their teams to facilitate buying decisions rather than push for sales. This means evolving how we structure Level 10 meetings, define Rocks, and measure success.

The Bridge to Growth

This pivot doesn't involve abandoning everything we know about sales. The fundamental human dynamics of decision-making remain the same, and EOS's powerful tools for creating organizational clarity and alignment remain.

What's changed is the context in which we operate. Buyer skepticism, commoditization, and the democratization of information have transformed the sales landscape. The Buyer-First Pivot is about adapting to this new reality.

When I made this shift in my own selling, the results were immediate and dramatic. Not just in the number of deals I closed (a record for my employer) but in all the dynamics of the sales process. Resistance dropped. Engagement increased. Sales cycles shortened. Most importantly, buyers and sellers found the process more satisfying and successful.

I've since helped dozens of companies make this same pivot. The results are consistent: When you stop pushing your perspective and start aligning with buyer reality, everything changes:

- Sales cycles shorten because you're working with the buyer's process, not against it.

- Win rates improve because you're solving for the buyer's needs, not your quota.

- Margins strengthen because you're demonstrating real value, not claiming it.

- Forecasts become reliable because they're based on buyer progress, not seller activity.

This isn't a theory or another sales methodology. It's a fundamental reorientation of how we approach B2B sales, aligned with how modern buyers make decisions.

In the coming chapters, we'll explore the four transformations needed to implement the Buyer-First Pivot and show how to evolve your sales process, messaging, people, and leadership to thrive in today's reality.

THE BUYER-FIRST SALES PROCESS

For decades, the Standard Sales Model has viewed selling as an activity that persuades prospects to buy. This model fixates on what salespeople do to move prospects through a predetermined sales process, coaxing agreements at each step from initial contact to proposal acceptance. However, this approach is outdated and counterproductive in today's hyper-competitive, commoditized markets.

The Buyer-First approach challenges traditional sales wisdom.

This might seem like a subtle shift in perspective, but make no mistake—its consequences are profound and far-reaching. It fundamentally alters how you approach every phase of your sales process, from initial contact to closing and beyond.

Instead of viewing sales as a persuasion game, we must reframe it as a collaborative process that helps the buyer succeed.

Consider the last time you were on the receiving end of a sales pitch. Did you feel the salesperson was genuinely interested in your success, or were you just another potential commission? Chances are, you could sense their true intentions, and it colored your entire interaction.

This is the crux of the matter. Human beings are incredibly adept at discerning the intentions of others. It's palpable when a salesperson is more motivated by making the sale than by ensuring the buyer's success. This implicit manipulation causes buyers to become defensive, skeptical, and more prone to objections—all of which work against both making the sale and helping the buyer succeed.

The Buyer-First Sales Process addresses this fundamental flaw in the Standard Sales Model. Aligning the salesperson's goals with the buyer's success creates an environment of trust and collaboration. This alignment is more than feel-good rhetoric. It's a strategic imperative in a world where buyers are more informed and skeptical and have more options than ever before.

To truly understand this system's power, we must explore its core components: mindset, process, and execution. Let's examine these and see how they combine to create a more effective, ethical, and sustainable sales process in today's challenging market.

Aligning Intentions for Mutual Success

A profound realization is at the heart of a Buyer-First Sales Process: buyers and sellers ultimately should want the same thing.

This might seem counterintuitive at first glance. After all, isn't the buyer trying to get the best deal while the seller aims to maximize profit?

But zoom out, and a different picture emerges. The buyer wants a solution that genuinely meets their needs and achieves the goals that initiated their search. While it's true that salespeople want to make the sale, experienced sales professionals know a fundamental truth: buyers rarely buy when sellers can't provide the right solution. When they buy a mismatched solution, it often ends in disaster.

These mismatched sales don't just result in unhappy customers. They damage your organization's reputation, hindering future sales and long-term growth. In today's interconnected world, where a single negative review can reach thousands of potential customers, a bad-fit sale costs more than ever.

These realizations lead to a crucial mindset shift. Instead of seeing the sales process as a battle of wills or a game to be won, it becomes a collaborative effort to find the best possible outcome for the buyer. This shift aligns the salesperson's intentions with the buyer's success, creating a foundation of trust crucial in today's skeptical market.

But this isn't just about feeling good or being nice. It's about results.

When buyers sense that you're genuinely invested in their success, they're more likely to open up about their real challenges, consider your insights seriously, and view you as a trusted advisor rather than just another vendor.

This mindset shift requires courage. It means being willing to walk away from deals that aren't a good fit, even if it means missing short-term revenue targets. It means investing time and resources into truly understanding the buyer's needs, even if there's a risk they might not buy from you in the end.

The payoff, however, is immense. When you consistently prioritize the buyer's success, you build a reputation as a trusted partner. This reputation becomes a powerful differentiator in a commoditized market, attracting high-quality prospects and making your sales process smoother and more predictable.

This mindset shift presents both a challenge and an opportunity for companies running on EOS.

The Buyer-First Sales Process fills this gap, aligning your internal excellence with your buyers' needs and perceptions.

Adopting this buyer-centric mindset sets the stage for a more effective sales process that aligns more with today's market realities.

While EOS excels at creating internal alignment and efficiency, it doesn't inherently address the buyer's perspective.

But mindset alone isn't enough. To revolutionize your sales approach, you need a process that embodies these principles at every step. Let's explore what that looks like.

The Process Imperative

Before we discuss the specifics of the Buyer-First Sales Process, let's address a crucial point: the importance of having a structured process in the first place.

Relying solely on individual salespeople's skills and intuition is a recipe for inconsistency and missed opportunities in today's complex sales environment. A well-designed, repeatable sales process is helpful and vital for both salesperson and organizational success.

A structured process ensures every prospect receives a consistent experience, regardless of which salesperson they interact with. This consistency is crucial for building and maintaining your brand reputation.

As your organization grows, a defined process allows you to onboard new salespeople more quickly and effectively. It provides a framework for new hires to follow as they develop their skills and learn the nuances of your market.

A standardized process allows you to measure performance at each stage, identify bottlenecks, and make data-driven improvements. It also creates a sales language for the leader and the team to use when discussing opportunities. The process names specific turning points in the buyer's journey. Without this structure, optimization becomes guesswork.

Buyers can sense when a salesperson is following a structured approach. It instills confidence that they're dealing with a professional organization, not just a charismatic individual. A defined process with clear stages and milestones establishes a pipeline that tracks the buyer's journey. When it begins tracking buyer decisions that predict sales, this pipeline becomes a scarily accurate sales forecast. Accurate forecasts are the ultimate tool for management because they empower you to plan your growth, allocate resources, and (finally) run your business confidently instead of reacting to surprises.

Most importantly, a well-designed sales process embeds decades of learning about selling and human behavior. A well-documented process captures your entire sales team's collective wisdom and best practices. It turns individual expertise into organizational knowledge. It makes each salesperson much more effective than relying solely on their intellectual, emotional, and relational skills.

Ultimately, it also increases your enterprise value. The difference between an acquirer paying you 4x EBITDA and 6x or more EBITDA for your business is the result of their confidence that they can duplicate your results. The difference between 4x and 6x is 50%. It's the difference between exiting with $10M and $15M, $30M and $45M or more. An effective, predictable, and proven sales process is often the number one factor driving that difference.

However, this is crucial because not all sales processes are created equal. The milestones tracked by your process must correspond to the forces that turn prospects into customers. Unlike the Standard Sales Model, where process milestones focus on seller activities, the Buyer-First Sales Process is crafted to reflect the buyer's journey.

This buyer-centric process can be divided into two main phases: Initiating and Qualifying (which focuses on the Buyer's Problem) and Winning and Growing (which addresses the solution and long-term relationship). Between these two phases lies a critical turning point.

Let's examine each of these elements in detail and see how they combine to create a sales process that is more effective and aligned with today's market realities.

Initiating & Qualifying

The first phase of the Buyer-First Sales Process concerns the buyer's problem.

It's tempting to pitch your solution immediately, but resist that urge. You can't truly help buyers succeed until you initiate a meaningful relationship and confirm that they have a problem you can genuinely solve.

This phase starts by determining whether there's a real opportunity to help. You need to assess whether the buyer has the correct issues that align with your solution. This isn't about forcing a fit but evaluating whether you can provide real value.

Once you've established that potential, you collaborate with the buyer to build a shared understanding of the problem. This process often uncovers nuances and complexities the buyer might not have been aware of or fully considered. These nuances and complexities are often so compelling to the buyer that they drive their purchasing decision.

Next, you need to validate the pain. Ensure the problem is significant enough to create urgency and motivate a buying decision. If the pain isn't acute, the buyer will likely not prioritize finding a solution.

At the same time, you need to understand the constraints that have prevented the buyer from solving the problem until now. These constraints often reveal critical information about the buyer's situation and decision-making process the Standard Sales Model never discovers.

Confirming resources is another crucial step at this point in the process. You must validate that the buyer has the necessary time, money, and organizational support to implement a solution. If these resources aren't available, pushing for a sale is counterproductive for both parties. It might boost your short-term numbers but will usually lead to dissatisfaction and damage your reputation in the long run.

Finally, perhaps most importantly, you must co-create the buying process with the buyer. This critical step is often overlooked in traditional sales approaches. Work with the buyer to determine who makes the decision, on what timeline, with input from which stakeholders, and according to what criteria.

Co-creating a buying process with your buyer uncovers hidden objections early and ensures the buyer feels ownership of the process, not manipulation.

The beauty of the Buyer-First Sales Process to the Initiating & Qualifying stage is that the answers to each question can be documented objectively. As a result, these milestones and whether the buyer has satisfied their requirements can be tracked and communicated. Even if there is some subjectivity, for example, to validate the buyer's problem, these milestones are at least as measurable as those in most traditional sales processes.

However, the benefit of tracking these milestones in preference to the standard sales model is that they are much closer to the buyer's journey. The milestones correspond to the factors determining whether you'll make the sale.

The result? Much more reliable forecasts. When your pipeline reviews track whether the conditions for sale are in place from the buyer's perspective, you get a clearer picture of your actual sales potential rather than just logging seller activities like meetings held or proposals sent.

This approach might seem time-consuming, especially compared to jumping straight into pitching. But it's an investment that pays enormous dividends. By thoroughly understanding the buyer's world before proposing a solution, you set the stage for a more effective and efficient sales process.

You also set yourself apart in our increasingly commoditized markets and begin to stand out for all the right reasons.

The Turning Point

Once you've completed the Initiating & Qualifying phase, you reach a critical juncture in the Buyer-First Sales Process: the turning point. This is a moment of decision for both buyer and seller, fundamentally different from anything in the Standard Sales Model.

In traditional sales approaches, the critical decision is often postponed until the end of the process, when the buyer has to decide whether to sign the contract and commit funds.

The Buyer-First Sales Process, in contrast, raises the stakes much earlier. You've validated that the problem exists and that the buyer is committed to solving it. You've confirmed that the buyer has the necessary resources to implement a solution. You've co-created a buying process that both parties agree on. Now, you and the buyer have a decision: do we proceed?

This early decision point can be scary for salespeople accustomed to the Standard Sales Model. Even if things look shaky, there's always hope you can rescue a deal later in the process. But creating this turning point early is vital. It recognizes that both buyer and seller will commit significant resources in time and money if they continue the process. Making this explicit decision point ensures that both parties are genuinely committed.

It's also a demonstration of respect for the buyer. Helping the buyer succeed means not wasting time if they're not fully committed to continuing. It's a demonstration of your integrity and commitment to their best interests.

From a sales efficiency standpoint, the painful reality is that we rarely can rescue a deal that can't commit to the process early on.

We'll never have more buying momentum than immediately after we've validated the problem, resources, and co-created process.

If that buying momentum isn't sufficient to convince the buyer to continue the process, it won't be sufficient to make the sale. And if a buyer can't commit to moving forward, gracefully exiting the deal at this stage frees up your organization's resources to focus on your best opportunities.

However, when buyers commit at this stage, your chances of making the sale increase dramatically. People are reluctant to reverse from such commitments.

This approach is superior to most EOS companies' standard selling process in several ways. While EOS provides a solid framework for internal operations, it doesn't adequately address the nuances of the buyer's journey.

The turning point in the Buyer-First Sales Process ensures that we are always aligned with the buyer's needs and readiness rather than pushing forward based solely on internal metrics or quotas.

Your conversion rate at this part of the process might decrease. It's almost certain your vanity metrics will suffer, at least initially. But the benefits you get for accepting this risk are substantial. The resources you free up by disqualifying poor-fit opportunities early result in more closed deals, more successful clients, fewer surprises, and less frantic activity later in the process. It's a night-and-day difference in terms of efficiency and effectiveness.

Winning & Growing

Once you've passed the turning point and both parties have committed to moving forward, you enter the Win & Grow phase of the Buyer-First Sales Process. This phase is more than just closing a deal—it's about setting the foundation for a long-term, mutually beneficial partnership.

The Win stage begins with defining the solution with the client. This can involve extensive specification and problem-solving to tailor your organization's knowledge, technology, and products to the client's unique needs in highly complex sales. In less complex sales, you might have a pre-built solution that's a good fit, and this part of the process is where you present that solution, following the buying process you co-created with the buyer.

Regardless of the complexity of the sale, once you've presented the solution, the buyer has to respond. There are three potential outcomes:

1. **The buyer decides to buy.** In this case, it's time to work with them on implementation, establish criteria to measure outcomes, validate your results, and grow the relationship. This follow-through is crucial in the Buyer-First Sales Process—your commitment to their success doesn't end when they sign the contract.

2. **The buyer says no.** While disappointing, this is an opportunity to work with them to discover where your solution fell short and understand why they chose a competitor's option (or not to buy at all). This information is invaluable for improving your offering and your process.

3. **The buyer refuses to make a decision.** In these cases, the Buyer-First Sales Process requires you to co-create a process with the buyer that ends in having what they need to make a concrete yes/no decision. This approach respects both parties' time and resources.

This process is superior to the Standard Selling Model and EOS in several ways. By co-creating the buying process and solution definition, you ensure you're always moving in step with the buyer's needs and decision-making process. The clear decision points and co-created processes eliminate the "black box" feeling many buyers experience with traditional sales approaches.

In my experience, co-creating the buying process with the buyer also removes many of the obstacles that delay a typical sales process. Buyers understand that our reputations are our currency in the marketplace. Like most honest people, they usually are reluctant to lose face by betraying their commitments.

In making the buyer to commit early to a decision-making process—without a whiff of manipulation, coercion, or any of the standard sales tactics—the buyer-first sales process also underscores just how much time, effort, and intention your team is investing in helping them succeed. The result is to foster a social and psychological context that naturally advances the buying process.

Securing buy-in at multiple stages then creates a sense of partnership and shared responsibility for the outcome. The feedback loop built into this process, even in the case of lost deals, provides valuable insights for improving your offering and approach. This process emphasizes implementation, measurement, and relationship growth, setting the stage for long-term partnerships rather than one-off transactions.

This approach offers a powerful antidote for companies grappling with the crisis of commoditization discussed earlier. It differentiates you not only on your product or service but also on the entire buying experience. It positions you as a trusted advisor and partner, not just another vendor in a sea of similar options.

The Buyer-First Imperative

In today's hyper-competitive, increasingly commoditized market, the Buyer-First Sales Process isn't just a nice-to-have—it's a strategic imperative.

This approach addresses the core challenges facing sales organizations today. By focusing on the buyer's unique needs and co-creating solutions, you differentiate yourself in ways that go beyond features and price. The transparency and collaboration inherent in this process build trust, overcoming the natural skepticism of today's buyers.

By co-creating the buying process, you can more effectively navigate the complexities of modern B2B purchasing decisions. The clear decision points and early qualification process ensure that you're investing your resources in the opportunities most likely to succeed. Aligning your process with the buyer's journey also gives you a clearer picture of your true sales potential, leading to more accurate forecasts.

The benefits of this approach extend far beyond individual deals. Organizations adopting the Buyer-First Sales Process see shorter sales cycles as buyers move through the process more confidently and commit. They experience higher win rates as they focus their efforts on well-qualified opportunities. Customer satisfaction and loyalty increase, leading to more repeat business and referrals. Team morale improves as salespeople feel aligned with a higher purpose beyond just hitting quota.

However, implementing this approach requires more than just a change in process. First and foremost, it requires a profound mindset shift for sales leadership and the sales team. It also demands a fundamental shift in how you communicate with prospects and guide them through their buying journey.

In the next chapter, we'll explore how to craft a messaging system that supports this Buyer-First Sales Process, ensuring that every interaction moves you closer to a mutually beneficial partnership.

The choice is clear. You can continue with the standard approach, fighting an uphill battle against commoditization and buyer skepticism. Or you can embrace the Buyer-First Sales Process, revolutionize your team's sales approach, and position your company for long-term success in even the most challenging markets.

The time to act is now. Your competitors are already seeking new ways to stand out in a crowded market. By adopting the Buyer-First Sales Process, you can get ahead of the curve and establish your company as the go-to solution for your ideal customers. Don't let this opportunity pass you by. Your sales team—and your bottom line—will thank you.

Overcoming the
Messaging Muddle

Your message isn't just important—it's the most critical factor in your sales success.

This isn't hyperbole; it's the cold, hard truth of modern sales.

In today's hyper-competitive marketplace, your secret weapon is a compelling message that resonates with your customers' primary wants and needs. It's the key to unlocking attention, building trust, and persuading prospects to buy. But when your message is off, even by a fraction, you quickly become another voice in a deafening chorus of sameness.

What you say to prospects and in what order you say it determines whether you'll close the deal or lose it to a competitor.

The harsh reality is that most companies are flying blind regarding messaging. They might have cobbled together an elevator pitch and a handful of scripts, but virtually every company I've spoken with over the last fifteen years lacked a comprehensive, tested messaging suite that they know works. Instead, they're leaving their salespeople to fend for themselves, operating under the misguided assumption that crafting effective messages is part of a salesperson's innate skill set.

This approach is a recipe for disaster. It leads to inconsistent results, missed opportunities, and a sales team constantly reinventing the wheel. Worse, it leaves your company vulnerable to the whims of individual salespeople's communication styles and personal biases.

The cost of this messaging neglect is staggering. How many deals have slipped through your fingers because your message didn't resonate? How many potential customers have you lost to competitors simply because their story was more compelling than yours? If you could calculate them, the numbers would likely keep you up at night.

The good news, however, is that the right messaging approach can dramatically improve this situation. You can arm your sales team with a message so powerful and perfectly attuned to your ideal customers' needs and desires that it cuts through the noise and compels action. This isn't just about closing more deals—it's about transforming your entire sales operation into a finely tuned machine that consistently attracts and converts your ideal customers.

The Three Phases of Sales Messaging

The Three Phases of Sales Messaging

Overcoming Obstacles

Closing the Gaps

Setting the Frame

To master the art of sales messaging, you need to understand that it unfolds in three distinct phases: setting the frame, closing the gaps, and overcoming obstacles. Each phase is critical and requires a unique approach. Neglect any one of them, and your entire sales process can crumble.

Setting the frame happens in the crucial first moments of contact with a prospect. This is where you make—or break—that all-important first impression. Get this right, and you set the stage for a productive conversation that can lead to a closed deal. Get it wrong, and you'll fight an uphill battle for the rest of the sales process.

Closing the gaps involves addressing the prospect's knowledge deficits. You educate them about your solution and their problem—often in ways they haven't considered before. This phase is where you build trust and credibility, positioning yourself as a vendor and a valuable partner in their success.

Overcoming obstacles is the final step toward a sale. In this process, you address objections head-on, solidify your value proposition, and call the prospect to action. It's a delicate dance that requires finesse, persistence, and a deep understanding of buyer psychology.

Mastering these three phases creates a smooth, logical progression that guides prospects from initial interest to signed contract. But make no mistake—this isn't about manipulation or pushy sales tactics. It's about aligning your message perfectly with your ideal customer's needs, and saying 'yes' becomes the obvious choice.

Let's dive deeper into these phases and uncover the secrets to crafting messages that sell.

The Sifter Message

The Sifter Message Framework

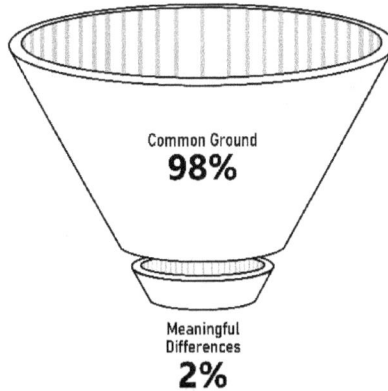

Common Ground
98%

Meaningful
Differences
2%

The adage that you never get a second chance to make a first impression holds doubly true in sales. What you say in the first five minutes of talking with a prospect, whether you're making a cold call or responding to a warm inquiry, will shape your entire relationship with this prospect.

For decades, the standard sales model has taught us to emphasize features and benefits immediately. We've been trained to use positioning statements to differentiate our product and place it in the best possible light from the very start. And for the better part of 80 years, this approach worked well.

But times have changed. As this approach has become standard practice, its effectiveness has plummeted. The reality of commoditization means it's now incredibly difficult to persuade prospects that you're different in ways that truly matter to them.

So, what do you do when the old playbook no longer works? You flip the script entirely. This is where the Sifter Message comes into play.

Yes, you read that right. Instead of immediately trying to stand out, you acknowledge the common ground.

The Sifter Message™ starts by doing something counterintuitive: it emphasizes how you're the same as your competitors.

Let me share a personal story to illustrate this point. Years ago, when selling security services, I faced a significant challenge. Our company was relatively unknown, competing against industry giants with huge marketing budgets and decades of brand recognition. Every sales call felt like an uphill battle.

One day, frustrated with another prospect dismissing us as "just another security company," I decided to try something different. Instead of launching into our unique selling points, I opened the call by saying, "You're right. 98% of what I do is exactly the same as Big Competitor 1 and Big Competitor 2. Codes and compliance require this. So, can we discuss the 2% that might matter to you and your team?"

The prospect, clearly taken aback, stopped trying to end the call. For the first time in weeks, I had someone's full attention. I continued, "We believe that real security isn't just about responding to incidents—it's about preventing them in the first place. And that's where our unique approach comes in."

From there, I could explain our proactive security measures, advanced training programs, and commitment to tailoring our services to each client's needs. By first acknowledging the industry standards, I had leveled the playing field. We were no longer perceived as small players trying to compete with the big boys— we were a company confident enough in our unique value to admit where we were similar.

This approach, which I've since refined and named the Sifter Message, works because it addresses the reality of commoditization head-on. It builds trust by aligning with the prospect's existing perceptions and redirecting their attention to the differences that truly matter.

But the Sifter Message doesn't stop there. After establishing common ground and highlighting meaningful differences, it does something revolutionary in sales: it describes who should not buy your product or service.

Yes, you read that correctly. The Sifter Message actively discourages specific prospects from buying. This might sound like sales suicide, but it's a powerful tool for focusing your efforts on the right customers.

You accomplish two crucial things by clearly stating who your offering is best for. First, you build trust by demonstrating honesty and confidence in your offering. Second, you begin to sift poor-fit prospects from ideal customers early, saving time and resources that would otherwise be wasted on leads that never convert.

This approach is the antithesis of the standard sales model, which focuses on increasing conversion rates at the early stages of the sales process. While it might seem intuitive that convincing more leads to enter your sales process will result in more customers, the reality is far different.

Every prospect you entice into your process, who isn't a good fit, will drain far more resources than you'll ever get in return.

56

They make your sales pipeline look full when, in reality, you have a lot of prospects who are likely never to buy or, worse, likely to become problem customers should they buy.

The Sifter Message solves this problem by qualifying prospects from the first interaction. It ensures that the leads entering your pipeline are numerous, high-quality, and aligned with your offering.

Implementing the Sifter Message requires courage. It means being willing to turn away potential business in the short term to build a stronger, more profitable customer base in the long term. But it's a game-changer for businesses ready to break free from the commodity trap and establish themselves as true partners to their ideal customers.

Closing the Gaps

Your job fundamentally changes once you've successfully used the Sifter Message to bring a qualified prospect into your sales process. You're no longer trying to sell. Instead, you're helping them make a good buying decision. This shift

The hard truth is that prospects often fail to buy desperately needed solutions because of gaps in their knowledge.

in mindset is at the heart of the Buyer-First Pivot, and it's crucial for success in today's skeptical, information-saturated market.

This is contrary to what many salespeople believe. This reason is rarely because the prospect doesn't want the solution or can't afford it.

These gaps can take many forms. Sometimes, prospects labor under false beliefs about your product category or specific offering. Other times, they simply haven't learned what they need to know to make a wise decision. Your job in this phase is to uncover and fill these gaps with the correct information.

This is where the real work of sales begins. You need to become part detective, part educator, and part consultant. You're not just presenting information—you're guiding your prospects through a journey of discovery that leads them to the right decision for their needs.

Start by digging into your prospect's situation. What are their pain points? What solutions have they tried before? What do they think they know about your offering or your industry? Only by understanding where they're starting from can you effectively guide them to where they need to be.

Once you've identified the gaps, your next task is to close them. This isn't about dumping information on your prospect. It's about strategically sharing insights that challenge their thinking, introduce new ideas, and reframe their understanding of their problem and potential solutions.

This approach goes far beyond the EOS concept of showcasing a "proven process." While demonstrating your process is valuable, it's not enough in today's market. You must be a thought leader and trusted advisor, not just another vendor with a good track record.

In practice, this phase often involves several touchpoints. You might deliver a series of presentations, each building on the last. You might provide documentation that addresses specific concerns or misconceptions. You might offer demonstrations that prove the effectiveness of your solution in contexts relevant to your prospect.

Tailoring each interaction to your prospect's specific situation and knowledge gaps is vital. Cookie-cutter presentations won't cut it. You need to be responsive, adaptive, and focused on helping your prospect clearly understand their problem and your solution.

This approach requires significant time and effort, but the payoff is enormous. By guiding prospects through this educational journey, you position yourself as a true partner in their success.

You build trust and credibility, leading to closed deals, long-term partnerships, and glowing referrals.

Remember, in the Buyer-First Pivot, your goal isn't just to make a sale. Your goal is to ensure that every customer you acquire is well-informed, confident in their decision, and primed for success with your solution.

This approach might seem to slow down your sales process. However, it most often accelerates it by eliminating the hesitation, second-guessing, and eleventh-hour objections plaguing many traditional sales efforts.

The Final Push

As you near the end of the sales process, you enter the crucial phase of overcoming obstacles and calling your prospect to action. In B2B sales, this often involves more than convincing a single decision-maker. You must create internal alignment among multiple stakeholders, each with their own concerns and priorities.

This phase requires a messaging system with several key components, each designed to address specific challenges in the final stages of the buying decision.

First, you need process messages. These are standard communications designed to move deals forward and challenge prospects to decide whether to commit or opt out. They create momentum and prevent deals from stalling in limbo.

For example, after a product demonstration, you might send a message recapping the key points, reiterating the value proposition, and asking the prospect to choose between scheduling a follow-up call or removing themselves from your pipeline. This kind of message respects the prospect's time while pushing for a clear next step.

Second, you need talking points that address common objections head-on. By anticipating and preparing for these objections, you can handle them smoothly and confidently when they arise. This preparation turns potential roadblocks into opportunities to reinforce your value.

For instance, if you sell a premium product or service, it's virtually guaranteed that your buyer will object to your price at some point during the Final Push. Without a well-developed messaging system, virtually every salesperson I've worked with in my career will be tempted by how close the finish line seems and try to overcome the price objection by negotiating.

This is almost always a mistake. You deserve to command a premium price if you have a premium product. Knowing that price will be an issue during the Final Push, you must develop a talking point that acknowledges the required investment, reframes it in terms of ROI, and provides concrete examples of how your solution pays for itself over time. The key is to address the objection early and directly, not dodge or dismiss it.

Most organizations try to solve this category of messaging problem with scripts. The problem with scripts is that the buyer doesn't know their lines. So when the salesperson launches into their objection handling script, the conversation quickly goes off the rails.

Talking points, however, can be inserted into any conversation in a manner that suits the situation and the salesperson's personality. You can think of the difference between scripts and talking points like the difference between a symphony and jazz. To successfully play a symphony, you need a conductor and everyone following the script. However, once musicians know a chord chart for a jazz tune, they can improvise a performance in virtually any context.

Finally, you need messaging that positions your offer, highlights its value, and calls prospects to action. This is where you combine everything you've communicated throughout the sales process into a compelling case for buying now.

Effective closing messages balance urgency with understanding. They push prospects toward a decision without being pushy. They reinforce the unique value you offer and the costs of inaction. And they provide a clear, easy path to saying "yes."

For example, your closing message might recap the prospect's key pain points, summarize how your solution addresses each one, highlight the potential ROI, and offer a limited-time incentive for acting quickly. The goal is to make the value of moving forward immediately crystal clear.

In crafting these messages, remember that B2B sales often involve multiple decision-makers. Your messaging needs to provide your champion within the organization with the tools they need to sell your solution internally. This might include executive summaries, ROI calculators, or comparison charts demonstrating your value proposition.

Preparation and personalization are the keys to success in this phase. Generic closing scripts won't cut it. You must tailor your messages to each prospect's concerns, priorities, and decision-making processes. This requires a deep understanding of the prospect's business, industry, and individual stakeholders.

Mastering this final messaging phase increases your chances of closing deals. More importantly, you ensure that when prospects say "yes," they do so confidently and enthusiastically, setting the stage for a successful long-term partnership.

The Buyer-First Advantage

The Buyer-First Pivot revolutionizes sales messaging. It acknowledges the reality of commoditization while still highlighting your actual value. It builds trust by aligning with buyer perceptions and then guides them to see your unique worth.

This approach creates messages that attract ideal prospects while repelling poor fits. It focuses your efforts on those most likely to become successful customers and positions you as a trusted advisor rather than just another vendor.

By mastering the three phases of sales messaging—setting the frame with the Sifter Message, closing the gaps through guided discovery, and overcoming obstacles with targeted, personalized communication—you create a smooth, logical progression from initial contact to a closed deal. This systematic approach takes the guesswork out of sales communications and drives consistent results.

In a world of increasing commoditization and buyer skepticism, the Buyer-First messaging approach gives you a powerful edge. It's not about being all things to all people—it's about being the perfect solution for the right people. And that's the key to sustainable sales success in today's challenging market.

Implementing this approach requires courage, effort, and a willingness to challenge conventional sales wisdom. But it's nothing short of transformative for businesses ready to break free from the commodity trap and establish themselves as true partners to their ideal customers.

The choice is yours. You can continue with the standard approach, fighting an uphill battle against commoditization and buyer skepticism. Or you can embrace the Buyer-First Pivot, revolutionize your sales messaging, and position your company for long-term success in even the most challenging markets.

The time to act is now. Your competitors are already seeking new ways to stand out in a crowded market. By adopting the Buyer-First messaging approach, you can get ahead of the curve and establish your company as the go-to solution for your ideal customers. Don't let this opportunity pass you by. Your sales team—and your bottom line—will thank you.

Hiring & Retaining
a Buyer-First Sales Team

O f all the frameworks EOS has made famous, its guidance on hiring may be the most powerful: "Right Person, Right Seat" and the "GWC" test. Gets it. Wants it. Has the Capacity to do it. Simple. Clear. And for most roles in your company, incredibly effective.

Think about your operations team, finance department, or customer service representatives. GWC works because it asks the three questions that matter most: Do they understand their role and your company? Are they motivated to succeed? Do they have the skills to do the job?

This framework has likely saved you from countless hiring mistakes. It's probably helped you build most of your current team. And when someone isn't working out, GWC helps you figure out why: they either don't get it, don't want it, or can't do it.

But there's a problem.

Your sales team keeps underperforming despite using this same framework. You hire people who seem to get it, clearly want it, and show every sign of being able to do it. Yet months later, they're struggling. Or worse, you're keeping them on because replacing them feels even riskier.

What's going on?

The problem isn't with GWC itself. The problem is that we're asking the wrong questions about sales roles. We're looking inward when we should be looking outward.

EOS tests for company fit when we should test for buyer fit.

We're evaluating their ability to work with us when we should be evaluating their ability to work with them.

And in today's brutal sales environment, this inside-out hiring approach costs you dearly.

Living a Buyer's World

Your accountant never has to convince someone to look at a spreadsheet. Your operations team doesn't face daily rejection from the production line. Your

The harsh reality is that your sales team faces a challenge no other employee in your company faces—and this changes everything about how you need to think about GWC.

IT department isn't fighting to get past gatekeepers just to fix a server.

But your sales team? They live in a different world.

Every day, your sales team faces people actively trying to say no to them. Buyers are trained to deflect their calls, dodge their questions, and delay their deals. Your prospects have read the same sales books your team has. They've been through negotiation training. They know every closing technique in the book—and how to counter it.

This fundamental difference exposes the flaw in how most EOS companies implement GWC for sales roles. The standard EOS training leads companies to test whether candidates understand internal processes, align with company values, and fit the culture. These matter for every role, but for sales positions, they're secondary to the skills and characteristics needed to succeed in your buyer's world.

No one tries to steal your secretary's stapler. But everyone tries to steal your salesperson's commission.

When you use GWC to evaluate sales candidates the same way you evaluate every other position, you're setting them up for failure. Your inside-the-company focus misses the crucial question: Can this person succeed in your buyer's world? This mismatch can devastate your growth in today's market, where buyers have more power than ever.

The Inside-Out Trap

You've probably felt the following sinking feeling. The promising sales hire who interviewed brilliantly is struggling six months in. They got along great with your team during interviews. They had years of industry experience. Your gut told you they were perfect. Yet here you are, watching another sales hire fail to deliver.

This pattern repeats in EOS companies because traditional hiring approaches focus on the wrong things.

We prioritize "culture fit" because we want someone who works well with our team. On the surface, this makes sense. But your best salespeople often create tension with operations precisely because they fight for their customers. They push for faster delivery, better terms, and special accommodations. The diplomatic candidate who never rocks the boat internally might be the wrong person to advocate for your buyers.

We value "industry experience" because we want someone who understands our business. However, a salesperson who has sold payroll systems to small businesses for ten years isn't automatically qualified to sell payroll systems to CFOs of mid-sized companies. The skills, approach, and buyer dynamics are completely different. What matters isn't industry experience—it's experience selling to your type of buyer.

We run comfortable, friendly interviews because that's how we evaluate every other role. But your buyers won't be relaxed and friendly. They'll challenge your salespeople, push back on pricing, and test their resolve. I once watched a company hire a $350,000-a-year salesperson based on pleasant conversations, only to discover they crumbled under pressure from actual buyers.

Most devastatingly, we trust our gut because it's worked for other hires. However, sales candidates are professional relationship builders. Valuing their ability to sell themselves in an interview is like being impressed that a chef can cook their signature dish. It tells you nothing about their ability to succeed with your buyers, in your market, and with your offering.

The cruel irony?

The better someone interviews in a traditional process, the less likely they are to succeed in today's brutal sales environment.

The traits that make someone shine in your conference room often work against them in your buyer's world.

This inside-out approach to hiring isn't just costing you salaries and time. It's costing you growth. Every month a mismatched sales hire stays on your team is a month of missed opportunities, stalled deals, and lost revenue.

There's a better way. But first, we need to understand exactly how this inside-out thinking distorts each element of the GWC framework.

The Buyers' Pivot for GWC

The concepts "right person, right seat" and "gets it, wants it, has the capacity to do it" are correct. However, we're asking the wrong version of each question for sales roles and collecting the wrong data. Let's examine what these elements mean in the buyer's world.

"Gets It" isn't about understanding your company's vision or values. It's about understanding how *your specific buyers* think and behave. Can your candidate ask the tough questions that make buyers uncomfortable—but lead to real solutions? Are they comfortable having direct conversations about money? Can they stay present and focused when a buyer pushes back or tries to derail the conversation?

These capabilities don't come from training. They stem from core beliefs about sales. Most of us grew up learning "don't talk about money," "don't ask too many questions," and "don't talk to strangers." Great salespeople must overcome these ingrained beliefs. When they don't, no amount of product training or sales techniques will help.

"Wants It" goes far beyond wanting the job or believing in your product. It's about having the will to sell. Every day, your sales-people face rejection. Every day, they must pick up the phone, knowing the person on the other end probably doesn't want to talk to them. Every day, they need to risk relationships by asking tough questions and pushing for decisions.

This requires a rare level of commitment, responsibility, and motivation. That's why the standard interview question, "Are you motivated to succeed?" is meaningless. Of course, they'll say yes. The real question is whether they have the emotional resilience and drive to pursue tough deals day after day.

"Capacity" isn't about being "good at sales." That phrase is meaningless without context. The skills needed to maintain eight accounts worth $10 million differ entirely from those required to grow those accounts to $15 million. And both differ in the skills needed to build a territory from scratch.

GWC EVOLUTION
Use Real Data to Understand GWC

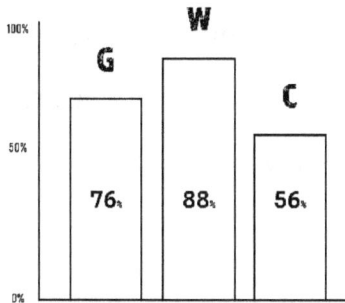

You need to define what success looks like in your specific sales role. What kinds of buyers will they face? What objections are common in your market? What decision-making processes will they need to navigate? Only then can you evaluate whether a candidate has the right capabilities—
or the potential to develop them.

Yet most companies do the opposite. They hire for product knowledge or industry experience, then wonder why their salespeople can't close deals.

It's much easier to train someone on your product than to train them how to sell.

I'm convinced the conventional wisdom about industry experience is a myth. What truly matters isn't whether a salesperson knows your specific industry—it's whether they understand and can relate to your buyer. Consider this: a Facilities Director regularly makes purchasing decisions about furniture, cleaning services, fire alarm systems, security systems, and HVAC maintenance. Each product is different, but they're all sold to the same person, who approaches buying decisions with consistent patterns and concerns.

The key is finding candidates who have successfully sold comparably complex or high-value solutions to your type of buyer, regardless of the specific product. A salesperson who has effectively sold security systems to Facilities Directors already understands the decision-making process, common objections, and organizational dynamics. They can leverage this buyer-centric experience and their rolodex of potential customers while learning your product's features and benefits. This perspective aligns perfectly with a buyer-first approach—instead of asking, 'What industry has this person worked in?' ask, 'Who have they sold to, and how well do they understand our buyer's world?'

The backwards inside-out approach most companies take to GWC explains why so many sales hires fail. We test for internal alignment when we should test for buyer alignment, and we evaluate their fit with us when we should evaluate their fit with them.

The Real Cost of Inside-Out Hiring

For most EOS companies, these questions reveal an uncomfortable truth. You're keeping underperformers because having anyone make sales calls feels better than having no one. You know they're not delivering the growth you need. But the thought of starting over, of risking another hiring mistake, feels worse than maintaining the status quo.

Take a hard look at your sales team. How many of the last five people you hired are still with you? How many performed at or above your expectations when you hired them? Most importantly, how many would you hire again knowing what you know now?

This fear creates a devastating cycle. You keep mediocre performers because you're not confident in hiring better ones. Meanwhile, each month of underperformance compounds your growth problem. Your competitors get stronger. Your market position weakens. The pressure to hit your revenue targets intensifies.

The real cost isn't the salary you're paying underperformers. It's not even the time and resources wasted on failed hires. The actual cost is the growth you're missing—growth that's going to your competitors.

When you make a bad sales hire, you lose far more than 12 months of salary and benefits. You lose:

- 3-6 months while you figure out they're not working out

- Another 3-6 months hoping they'll improve with training

- 2-3 months going through the hiring process again

- 3-4 months getting the new hire up to speed

That's 18 months of lost opportunity. Eighteen months where your territory isn't growing. Eighteen months where your competitors are taking market share. Eighteen months you can never get back. Not to mention the soft costs of a bad hire like damage to your reputation in the marketplace, loss of share of wallet, and apathy in your customer base.

And that assumes you get it right on the second try.

Most EOS companies know what they want their sales team to achieve. You have clear revenue targets, defined markets, and goals for growth. But if you can't confidently hire people to hit those targets, your otherwise excellent operating system has a fatal flaw.

The solution isn't to abandon EOS. The solution is to redefine how we evaluate sales candidates in today's market. We need a process that tests candidates the way buyers will test them, not the way we wish we could hire them.

Start With Capabilities

Traditional hiring processes, especially in my experience at EOS-managed companies, don't take GWC seriously enough. And they use the wrong tools to qualify that candidates get it, want it, and have the capacity to do it.. Let me explain.

Traditional hiring processes start by reading resumes, getting influenced by names, pictures, or experiences with competitors we admire (or hate). We tell candidates all about the wonderful opportunity before we know if they're qualified. We sell the position when we should be testing their capabilities.

The buyer-first approach turns this process on its head. Don't read their resume until you've tested their sales capabilities. Don't tell them about the specific role until you've verified they can sell. Don't worry about whether they'll accept your offer until you're sure you want to make one.

Most hiring managers and business owners also fail to consider the specific mix of sales skills and personality traits required for a particular sales position.

Every sales position demands a different mix of capabilities. Maintaining existing accounts requires deep relationship skills, attention to detail, and the ability to spot expansion opportunities while keeping competitors at bay. Growing existing accounts requires those relationship skills, plus the ability to navigate complex buying committees, challenge comfortable relationships, and push for bigger commitments.

But building a territory from scratch demands a different skill set: hunter instincts, comfort with constant rejection, and the ability to create opportunities where none exist.

The good news? Once you identify the specific capabilities needed to succeed in your particular role, you can measure whether candidates have those skills—or the capacity to develop them.

This isn't guesswork. The assessment tools I use have been tested on millions of candidates over 35 years, with a 91% success rate at predicting success in specific sales roles. These aren't your typical personality tests that tell you whether someone is outgoing or detail-oriented. They measure the 21 core sales capabilities that determine success or failure in different sales roles.

Want to know if a candidate can handle tough price negotiations? There's data for that. Need someone who can navigate complex buying committees? We can measure that capability. Looking for someone who can build trust quickly with C-suite executives? That's measurable too.

You don't need to rely solely on data. I pair quantitative assessments with an initial ten-minute screening interview. By asking the right questions, you can quickly determine whether a candidate has what it takes to GWC the position you're hiring.

Quantitative assessments and the ten-minute interview don't just tell you whether to hire someone. They show you exactly what gaps you'll need to fill if you hire them. Instead of discovering their weaknesses six months in, you'll know them before you make an offer—and have a plan to address them.

No candidate is perfect. However, with the right data, you can identify candidates with the core capabilities you need and then develop the rest.

Test Candidates Like a Buyer

Now that you've identified the candidates that GWC your position, it's time to interview them fully. However, the right approach to interviewing candidates for sales roles differs significantly from what you might expect.

Want to know the fastest way to spot a bad sales hire? Look at how they handle their first challenge from you.

Every resume contains BS. Your job in the interview isn't to be impressed by their experience—it's to figure out where the BS is and see how they handle it when you call them out. Push back on their claims. Challenge their success stories. Question their numbers.

Does that sound uncomfortable? Too bad. Your buyers will be even tougher on them. If they wilt under your questioning, they'll crash and burn with your buyers.

Remember: Your sales candidates are professional relationship builders. Of course, they'll impress you in a friendly interview. Of course, they'll say all the right things about your company and opportunity. That's what salespeople do. But being good at selling themselves tells you nothing about their ability to succeed with your buyers.

Instead, make your initial interview challenging. Create scenarios that mirror real sales situations. Push them out of their comfort zone—not to be cruel but realistic. This isn't just about testing their skills. It's about testing their resilience, ability to think on their feet, and capacity to handle pressure.

The right candidates will rise to these challenges, and the wrong ones will reveal themselves before you waste months watching buyers make their limitations painfully apparent to anyone with eyes to see.

Hire With a Plan

In 2008, a fire alarm company hired me during the financial crisis. The job market was terrible, and the company thought it had leverage. It was wrong.

On day one, I showed up ready to sell. Instead, I spent the morning waiting, as no one seemed to know what to do with me. Finally, the VP of Sales handed me three technical manuals about alarm systems. "We have a technical product," he explained. "Learn these."

By the end of day two, I had walked into his office and resigned. If other jobs had been available, I would have been gone. However, the poor job market motivated me to negotiate a different approach. They needed a top performer, and I needed a job. We could work together—but only with the right plan.

Most companies are always trying to hire the perfect sales candidate. EOS inadvertently reinforces this quest with the seeming ease of "right person, right seat" and GWC. The painful truth is that the perfect sales candidate doesn't exist. Instead, if you want the perfect person in the perfect seat, you must create that match. You do that by starting with the right raw materials and having a clear development plan for your new hire.

Eight months later, I was the company's top-performing salesperson. This was not because I memorized technical manuals or had industry experience but because we developed a buyer-first message and sales process that made the most of the excellent sales skills I already possessed.

I'm the exception. Most salespeople would have failed in that situation. Not because they lacked talent but because the company had no plan to make them successful. My employer was focused entirely on product knowledge when they should have been focused on selling capabilities.

This is why objective data matters so much. Not to find perfect candidates—they don't exist. But to identify exactly which gaps you can fill through training and development and which you can't. Create a plan that turns the right raw talent into your perfect fit.

Consider it this way: Your buyers will find your salespeople's weaknesses. Wouldn't you rather find them first and address them before they fail?

Your Next Sales Hire Is Too Important to Risk

EOS provided the right framework with GWC. However, knowing the framework isn't enough in today's brutal sales environment. You need a practical, proven way to evaluate sales candidates against the realities they'll face when they step into your buyer's world.

Your next sales hire represents more than just a salary. They represent months of market opportunity. Territory potential. Revenue growth. Or, if you get it wrong, months of stagnation while your competitors gain ground.

You can't afford to guess. You can't rely on gut feeling. And you certainly can't keep hiring the same way and expecting different results.

The good news? You don't have to reinvent your hiring process from scratch. You don't need to abandon GWC. You just need to evolve how you apply it to sales roles.

Start by asking yourself these questions:

Are you truly testing candidates the way your buyers will test them? Or are you running comfortable interviews that tell you nothing about their ability to succeed in tough sales situations?

Are you evaluating their fit with your buyers? Or are you focused solely on their fit with your internal team?

Do you have a concrete plan to develop the right candidate into your perfect fit? Or are you still searching for that mythical, ideal hire?

If you're ready to transform how you hire salespeople and build a sales team that can thrive in today's market, let's talk. We've helped dozens of companies evolve their approach to sales hiring, and we can help you too. There's information at the end of this book about how to get in touch.

Your next sales hire is too important to risk getting wrong. Let's make sure you get it right.

THE BUYER-FIRST SALES MANAGER

By now, you've seen how the buyer-first pivot transforms the sales process, messaging, and hiring. You've discovered why traditional approaches, focused on internal metrics and seller activities, fail in today's market. You've learned new frameworks for engaging buyers, crafting resonant messages, and identifying sales talent that can thrive in your buyers' world.

None of these transformations will stick without reimagining sales management.

Most sales managers are trapped in an inside-out paradigm. They spend their days scrutinizing pipeline reports, updating forecasts, and pushing their team to hit activity metrics. They run endless pipeline reviews focused on probability percentages. They track calls made, meetings held, and proposals sent. They serve the company's need for predictability and control.

Meanwhile, their buyers—who determine their success—remain abstract data points in a CRM.

This internal focus isn't entirely their fault. Most sales managers were promoted for being great salespeople and then left to figure out management on their own. They either default to managing how they were managed or try to make their team do what made them successful as individual contributors.

This challenge is particularly acute for companies running on EOS. Tools that bring clarity and alignment to other parts of your organization can reinforce the internal focus that undermines sales success. Your Level 10 meetings become pipeline reviews. Your scorecard tracks lagging indicators. Your issues list is filled with tactical sales problems rather than strategic opportunities.

The result? Your sales managers spend time serving the system rather than enabling their team to serve buyers. They become administrators rather than leaders, focused on reporting rather than developing the capabilities their team needs to succeed.

This misalignment can devastate your growth. When sales managers focus primarily inward, they miss their critical role in your buyer-first transformation. They fail to develop their team's ability to create value for buyers. They don't coach the sophisticated skills needed to navigate today's complex buying environments. They don't guide their team in crafting compelling buyer-focused strategies.

When Internal Excellence Isn't Enough

EOS is a powerful system that has transformed countless businesses by bringing clarity, alignment, and accountability to their operations. Yet when it comes to sales management, EOS has a significant blind spot.

The problem starts with Level 10 meetings. In most departments, the L10 format works brilliantly. The scorecard metrics perfectly track internal efficiency, and the issues list captures real problems that need solving.

However, the standard EOS approach reinforces all the wrong behaviors in sales.

These metrics tell you what happened last week or last month, but they don't help you understand what's happening with your buyers right now.

Your sales scorecard becomes a laundry list of lagging indicators: revenue booked, proposals sent, and meetings held.

Weekly sales meetings devolve into pipeline reviews, during which managers interrogate reps about probability percentages and close dates. The team then spends precious meeting time updating CRM data instead of developing strategies to help buyers succeed.

The issues list is filled with tactical problems: stuck deals, unresponsive prospects, competitive price pressure. While these issues feel urgent, discussing them one by one misses your market's broader patterns and strategic challenges.

Even the rocks system, so effective in other departments, can work against you in sales. Three-month goals make perfect sense for internal projects. But buyer decisions don't conform to your quarterly calendar. Setting rocks around revenue or closed deals can push your team to force deals through that aren't ready, damaging both buyer relationships and your company's reputation.

The problem isn't with EOS itself. The real problem is that we're trying to manage an external-facing, buyer-driven function with tools designed for internal operations.

Your operations team controls their production schedule. Your finance team controls their closing process. Your HR team controls their hiring timeline. But your sales team? They're at the mercy of buyer schedules, methods, and decisions.

This fundamental difference demands a different approach to management. You need a system that tracks leading indicators of buyer engagement, uses meeting time to develop buyer-focused strategies, addresses patterns and systemic issues, and aligns goals with buyer success.

You don't have to abandon EOS. You just need to evolve how you apply it to sales management.

Breaking the Pipeline Review Trap

Watch your sales manager for a week. They'll spend hours with your salespeople reviewing opportunities, updating close dates and probability percentages, pushing for next steps and commitments, and adjusting forecasts based on gut feel and historical patterns.

It's mind-numbing work. It's also pointless.

They tell you what happened but do nothing to improve what will happen. Your sales manager feels like they're managing the sales process when they're just documenting it.

Pipeline reviews, as most companies conduct them, are backward-looking exercises in data collection.

Look at your sales manager's calendar. How much time do they spend updating CRM fields versus developing strategies to help buyers succeed? In most organizations, the ratio is about 80/20—and not in the right direction.

Traditional approaches fail because more scrutiny doesn't lead to better forecasts. Forecast accuracy improves through better sales process and buyer alignment. Knowing that a salesperson sent a proposal tells you nothing about whether the buyer is moving toward a decision. Every minute your sales manager spends updating probability percentages is not spent developing the team's capabilities or crafting buyer-focused strategies.

You still need visibility into your sales pipeline and a way to forecast revenue. But your sales manager needs to flip the model on its head.

Instead of scrutinizing every deal, they should focus on patterns and systemic issues. Instead of updating data fields, they should guide discussions about buyer progress and obstacles. Instead of pushing for the next steps, they should help develop strategies to create value for buyers.

This means changing both the frequency and format of pipeline reviews:

Monthly Reviews: Deep dives into the full pipeline, focusing on patterns and strategic issues. What barriers are multiple buyers hitting? Where is the team creating value, and where are they falling short? What market changes are affecting buyer decisions?

Weekly Check-ins: Quick updates focused on immediate needs and opportunities. Which deals need strategic help this week? What resources could accelerate buyer progress? Where could coaching have the biggest impact?

This shift frees up time for your sales manager to reinvest in activities that drive growth. You'll feel less in control initially. Your leadership team might push back on less frequent detailed reviews.

Stand firm. Your sales manager isn't reducing oversight—they're increasing effectiveness.

The 60-20-10-10 Revolution

Most sales managers spend their time backward. They invest 80% of their energy in backward-looking activities like pipeline reviews and forecast updates. Then they wonder why their team isn't growing.

**The 60-20-10-10
Sales Management Model**

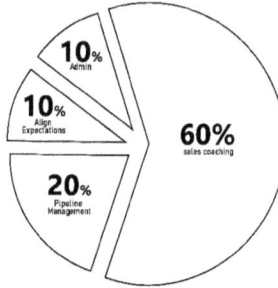

This is where growth happens.

Your sales manager should spend most of their time developing your team's capabilities and helping them craft winning strategies. Regular coaching sessions focus on skill development. Deal strategy sessions examine opportunities from the buyer's perspective. Field rides and call

Your sales manager needs to spend 60% of their time on coaching mindset, skills, and deal strategy.

reviews develop real capabilities, not check boxes. Team training builds a systematic understanding of your buyers' world.

20% on pipeline management and forecasting. You still need pipeline visibility, but your sales manager should focus on patterns and progress, not details and data entry. They should spot systemic issues affecting multiple deals, identify where buyers get stuck, and create reliable forecasts based on buyer behavior, not seller optimism.

10% on expectations, goals, and accountability. Clear standards matter but shouldn't consume the week. Your sales manager should set expectations aligned with buyer success, track meaningful metrics that drive the right behaviors, and address performance issues promptly.

10% on administrative tasks and leadership team interface. Every role has necessary administrative work. Keep it contained through streamlined reporting, automated routine tasks, and efficient team communication systems.

This time allocation drives effectiveness. When your sales manager spends most of their time developing their team and crafting buyer-focused strategies, your salespeople improve. They develop sophisticated skills needed in today's market and learn to create real value for buyers. Your pipeline becomes more reliable, and your growth becomes sustainable.

This shift requires conviction from you as a leader. Your sales manager will face pressure to spend more time on reports and reviews. Hold the line. Better forecasts and stronger results come through better coaching and strategy, not more administration.

Coaching for Buyer Success

If you have a competent sales manager, they likely schedule regular coaching sessions with your salespeople. They listen to calls. They do field rides. They hold one-on-one meetings. Yet, more often than not, all this activity fails to create consistent improvement in your sales team's performance.

Most sales managers coach the way they were coached, focusing on traditional sales techniques and closing strategies. They critique presentation skills, suggest closing lines, and teach objection-handling techniques.

The problem isn't the activity—it's the focus.

For your buyer-first pivot to succeed, your sales manager needs to coach to a different standard. Instead of focusing on sales tactics, they should develop your team's deeper capabilities. Your salespeople need to understand buyer psychology and navigate complex decision-making processes. They must learn to work with buying committees, balancing competing priorities and multiple stakeholders. Most importantly, they need to create value in every interaction.

This isn't just a different set of skills—it's a different mindset. Your sales manager isn't training people to close deals; they're developing consultants who help buyers succeed.

Traditional coaching sessions critique a salesperson's handling of price objections. Buyer-first coaching explores why price concerns the buyer. What value are they not effectively demonstrating? How could they better align the solution with the buyer's success metrics? Which stakeholders or decision criteria are they missing?

Most sales managers don't know how to coach this way. They've never been trained in buyer-first methodologies. They're trying to develop capabilities they haven't mastered themselves.

You may need to invest in your sales manager's development first. Most sales managers are promoted to the role because they are top performers in the field, not because they have stellar sales management skills. They rarely receive training that helps them develop the most critical skills that lead to success as a sales manager.

Today's sales managers must understand modern B2B buying decisions and how to create value for buyers throughout the buying process. They must also learn to identify and develop buyer-focused capabilities in others and adapt their coaching to different situations and skill levels.

Activity isn't an achievement. Regular coaching sessions mean nothing if they reinforce outdated approaches. Your sales manager must shift focus from seller behaviors to buyer outcomes, centering every conversation on creating more buyer value.

The Strategic Deal Review

Deal reviews, like coaching, too often focus on the wrong things.

Watch a typical deal review: The sales manager asks about the next steps and close dates. The salesperson defends their forecast. They discuss completed and planned activities. They update CRM fields. They move on to the next deal.

Real deal reviews are strategic working sessions focused on understanding and advancing the buyer's journey. Your sales manager should help the team see their deals from the buyer's perspective.

They should dig into fundamental questions that determine whether a deal will close. Has the team documented the buying process? Are they aligned with how the buyer defines success? Do they understand all stakeholders and their motivations? Are they creating real value at every step?

These answers reveal more about closing likelihood than any probability percentage. They also provide natural coaching opportunities. When your sales manager uncovers gaps in buyer understanding, they can develop the capabilities to fill those gaps.

Strategic reviews require deeper preparation. Your salespeople need to understand their buyers' situations and articulate the business case from the buyer's perspective. Your sales manager guides the discussion toward a deeper understanding. They explore stakeholder motivations, challenge stated decision criteria, and connect patterns across deals.

This approach develops your team's strategic thinking. They anticipate challenges, spot hidden opportunities, and build stronger relationships through a deeper understanding of buyers.

The time investment pays off. Consider the alternative: How much time does your team waste pursuing deals they don't understand? How many opportunities slip away from missed buyer signals? How many forecasted deals vanish in the final stages?

Strategic deal reviews prevent these problems by ensuring your team understands their buyers before investing significant resources. They provide early warning when deals go off track, allowing course correction while there's still time.

Managing Up

The hardest part of transforming sales management isn't implementing changes—it's maintaining them against traditional expectations. This challenge intensifies in EOS companies, where pressure for consistent reporting and measurable results can push sales managers back toward traditional methods.

Your leadership team wants certainty. They want reliable forecasts, predictable revenue, and clear metrics—all reasonable desires. However, most companies pursue certainty in ways that make sales results less predictable.

In weekly Level 10 meetings, your sales manager presents numbers. The leadership team scrutinizes the pipeline. Questions fly about specific deals and close dates. Your sales manager promises to push harder, follow up more frequently, and get better commitments.

You're pushing your sales manager to focus on exactly the wrong things. They leave thinking about next week's numbers instead of creating buyer value. They gather data instead of developing capabilities.

The solution is not abandoning accountability or metrics. Your sales manager must help the leadership team understand that predictable revenue comes from buyer success, not seller activity.

They should share insights about buyer patterns and market dynamics rather than just reporting numbers. Especially as you undertake your buyer-first pivot, their score cards should adapt to measure the growth in team capability and buyer value until you have enough experience with your new sales process to develop confidence in your new pipeline and forecasts.

Your sales manager must help the leadership team understand the leading indicators of sales success. Not calls made or proposals sent, but buyer engagement and progress. How many buyers collaborate on solution design? Where do buyers invest their time? How many buyers have agreed to a buying process with your team? Which deals show strong multi-stakeholder engagement?

This shift requires courage from your sales manager—and patience from you and your leadership team. The pressure to provide deal-specific certainty never ends.

Your sales manager must stand firm, demonstrating how buyer-first approaches lead to reliable forecasts and better results. Show how developing capabilities drive consistent performance better than pushing activity. Help the leadership team see sales as a strategic function focused on buyer success, not just a tactical function hitting numbers.

A Fractional Solution

Sometimes the hardest part of transformation isn't recognizing the need for change—it's acknowledging that your current leadership may not be equipped to drive it.

Your sales manager might excel at traditional pipeline management and activity tracking. But they might at present lack either the temperament or skills to guide your buyer-first pivot.

More often, I encounter EOS companies where the owner or an early employee remains in the seat of managing sales, even though that isn't their full-time responsibility or highest skill.

In either case, coming to the realization that there is a skill gap when it comes to navigating your buyer-first pivot presents an opportunity to reimagine how sales leadership works in your organization. Enter the fractional sales manager a solution perfectly aligned with EOS principles of getting the Right Person in the Right Seat.

Fractional leadership isn't a compromise. It's often the optimal solution for companies undertaking the buyer-first transformation. These leaders bring decades of experience implementing sophisticated sales methodologies across multiple industries. They've guided numerous companies through exactly the transformation you're contemplating. Most importantly, they know how to build systems that outlast their tenure.

The cost can feel steep at first glance. Paying $7,500 to $12,000 monthly for one or two days a week might seem excessive compared to a full-time sales manager's salary. But this view misses the fundamental value proposition. You're not just hiring a manager—you're accessing expertise that most EOS companies couldn't afford to bring on full-time.

The math becomes compelling when you look closer. You avoid the burden of benefits, unemployment insurance, and employer-side payroll taxes. The relationship focuses intensely on transformation rather than day-to-day management. Most importantly, fractional leaders often accomplish more in their limited time than full-time managers achieve in a standard week—because they're not trapped in the pipeline review cycle.

A fractional leader's impact extends far beyond their direct involvement. They establish systems that create permanent change. They develop capabilities in your existing team that persist after their engagement ends. They build processes aligned with buyer success that become part of your company's DNA. While a traditional sales manager might maintain the status quo, a fractional leader transforms your entire approach to sales.

The arrangement particularly suits companies with smaller sales teams—exactly where many EOS organizations find themselves. Your team might not need full-time sales leadership, but they desperately need sophisticated guidance to navigate today's buyer-driven market. A fractional leader provides the expertise you need at a scale you can sustain.

This solution also aligns perfectly with EOS's focus on accountability and results. Fractional leaders succeed only if they create lasting transformation. They can't hide behind activity metrics or blame market conditions. Their success depends entirely on building systems that work and capabilities that stick.

The key lies in understanding that fractional leadership isn't a permanent arrangement. It's a strategic investment in transformation.

The right fractional leader will make themselves unnecessary by building the systems, developing the capabilities, and instilling the mindset your team needs for long-term success in the buyer-first world. A good fractional sales leader will create a structure that helps you know what good sales leadership looks like for your company, and create the systems you will rely on when you replace them.

From Manager to Leader

The buyer-first pivot transforms every aspect of your sales organization. It reshapes processes, revolutionizes messaging, and redefines hiring. But nowhere is this transformation more profound than in sales management.

The shift from traditional management to buyer-first leadership reimagines the sales manager role. Your sales manager must evolve from a tactical supervisor focused on control into a strategic leader focused on capabilities and buyer success.

This evolution demands courage. It requires challenging conventional wisdom about sales management, prioritizing long-term capability development over short-term numbers, and standing firm when traditional pressures push toward old methods.

This courage needs wisdom. Your sales manager must understand that buyer-first leadership redefines accountability and doesn't abandon it. It measures what drives success, not just what's easy to count. It focuses oversight on what matters, not what's comfortable to track.

Your role will be crucial. Your sales manager needs your support, understanding, and protection. They need you to defend their coaching focus when others demand more pipeline reviews, back their strategic approach when the leadership team wants tactical updates, and champion buyer-first principles when traditional metrics tempt retreat.

The transformation rewards the effort. A true buyer-first sales leader develops deeper capabilities in their team. Their pipeline becomes reliable. Their forecasts gain accuracy. Most importantly, their customers achieve success.

This defines sales leadership today: not just hitting numbers but building teams that create lasting buyer value. Not just managing pipelines but developing people who navigate complex buying decisions. Not just reporting metrics but driving genuine transformation in your sales approach.

The choice is yours. You can maintain the status quo of control and compliance with unpredictable results or embrace transformation, supporting your sales manager in becoming a leader who drives sustainable success in today's buyer-driven market.

THE PATH FORWARD

Two companies I'm working with as we write this perfectly illustrate both the challenge and the opportunity of the buyer-first pivot.

The first company recognized the need for change. It agreed that its traditional sales approaches weren't working and committed to making the pivot. But when it came time for real transformation, it hesitated. It balked when it came time to invest in updated messaging, believing its traditional approach was good enough. It made surface changes to its sales process but resisted fundamental shifts in perspective. When the time came to evolve its team, it balked at making difficult decisions.

The result? Its sales continue to stagnate. Its team struggles with longer cycles, growing price pressure, and declining win rates. It's stuck in the same commoditization trap we've discussed throughout this book.

The second company embraced transformation fully. It didn't just understand the need for change—it committed to making it happen. Its team seized on the new buyer-first message and process. It put development plans in place for its people. It invested in targeted coaching to help strategize solutions for challenging buyers. Its sales manager received coaching too, and their growth has been extraordinary.

Today, it is confronted with a very different problem: Its sales team is exceeding its quota and leadership is scrambling to add extra capacity to fulfill all the new orders it is receiving.

Making Change Real

Let's be clear about what we've discovered. The commoditization crisis in B2B sales isn't just another market cycle or temporary challenge. It's a fundamental breakdown of how we sell. The

The difference was senior management's commitment to real transformation.

Standard Sales Model, which served us well for decades, now works against us. Every traditional sales approach—from our discovery questions to our value propositions, sales process, and management methods—creates more buyer resistance, not less.

More troubling, our attempts to fix this through traditional means only worsen it. Better training makes us more obviously "salesy." Better processes create more buyer resistance. Better messaging pushes us deeper into the sameness spiral. Even perfect execution of internal systems like EOS can't bridge the growing gap between our internal excellence and our market results.

The buyer-first pivot offers us a way forward. But understanding the need for change isn't enough. We need a practical path to transformation.

Where to Start

After helping numerous companies make this pivot, I've learned that most organizations should start with their message. A new buyer-first message delivers quick wins that build confidence and secure buy-in from skeptical sales teams. These early successes create momentum for the deeper changes required in your sales process, talent management, and leadership approach.

One crucial exception to this rule: If your team fundamentally lacks the skills necessary to succeed with a buyer-first approach, start with hiring. You need people capable of making this pivot before you can implement it successfully.

Think of your message as the tip of the spear. It breaks through buyer skepticism and creates opportunities for genuine engagement. But without the right people wielding it, even the best message falls flat.[1]

The Journey Ahead

Making this transformation isn't easy. It requires more than one or two quarters of rocks, sustained attention, and commitment. Just as adopting EOS requires fundamental changes in how you operate, the buyer-first pivot requires deep changes in how you sell.

You'll face resistance. Old habits die hard. The pressure of quotas and forecasts will tempt your team to revert to pushing rather than guiding. Inside-out thinking will try to reassert itself.

But the market isn't waiting. Every quarter we delay this transformation, the commoditization crisis deepens. Win rates continue to fall, sales cycles stretch longer, and margins erode. The gap between our internal excellence and our market results grows wider.

The good news? The transformation is possible. We've seen companies across industries make this pivot successfully. The key is committing fully to the change rather than trying to straddle both approaches.

---

1   For more information on developing a Sifter Message for your organization, you can download a PDF on the subject at: https://magnet.helixsalesdevelopment. com/the-sifter-message-ebook

The Time to Start Is Now

Some companies make this transformation on their own. Others seek outside help—just as they did with EOS implementation—to avoid common pitfalls and accelerate their progress. Either path can work. The critical factor isn't how you make the change but your commitment to making it real.

What matters is starting now. Begin with your message unless your team lacks fundamental capabilities. Build momentum through early wins. Use that momentum to drive deeper transformations in your process, people, and leadership approach.

Most importantly, commit fully to the pivot. Partial implementation isn't enough.

The transformation must be complete for the results to follow.

The choice—and the journey—is yours. But one thing is certain: The future belongs to companies that make this pivot successfully. The only question is whether your company will be one of them.

> *You can't be partially buyer-first anymore than you can be partially committed to EOS.*

Here's How to Get Help

For companies running EOS, the buyer-first pivot represents both an opportunity and a challenge. The opportunity lies in breaking free from commoditization and building truly differentiated sales capabilities. The challenge comes in making this transformation stick while maintaining the accountability and structure that makes EOS powerful.

This is why I've developed The Sales Integrator™—a system specifically designed to help EOS companies make this critical transition. It's not just another sales methodology. It's a complete framework for integrating buyer-first selling into your EOS implementation.

Implementation Roadmap
The Sales Integrator™ Journey

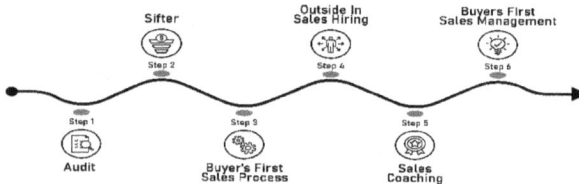

Think about your EOS journey. You could have read the books and implemented the system yourself. Many companies try. But making fundamental changes to how you operate is challenging. Under pressure, it's easy to revert to old habits. Without expert guidance, critical gaps in implementation often go unnoticed until they create serious problems.

The same challenges appear in the buyer-first pivot. Companies start strong, making surface changes to their sales approach. But old habits creep back in under the pressure of quotas and forecasts. Inside-out thinking reasserts itself. The team reverts to pushing rather than guiding. Gradually, imperceptibly, they slide back into the approaches they were trying to escape.

The Sales Integrator helps you avoid these pitfalls. It starts with the Sifter Message framework, transforming your Three Uniques from internally focused differentiators into compelling external value that resonates with buyers. This bridges the critical gap between how you see your value and how buyers perceive it.

In addition to developing a Sifter Message that attracts your ideal customers while repelling time-wasting tirekickers, we develop talking points that address common objections and tap into the hooks and levers buried deep in your prospects' psychology. These are written to help your team begin implementing best practices immediately while providing a system for getting new hires up to speed as soon as month one.

The Sales Integrator then helps align your sales process with your buyer's journey while maintaining the accountability and metrics that make EOS powerful. Instead of abandoning what works in EOS, you evolve it to support buyer-first selling.

Perhaps most importantly, The Sales Integrator helps you identify who on your team gets it, wants it, and can make this pivot. Not everyone necessarily will, so having a proven framework for evaluating and developing your team through this transformation is crucial for success.

Finally, it provides the tools and frameworks to transform your sales leadership approach. Your Level 10 meetings, Scorecard, and Rocks evolve to support buyer-first selling while maintaining the clarity and accountability that makes EOS work.

Taking the Next Step

Throughout this book, we've explored how traditional sales approaches fail in today's market. You've seen how even well-run EOS companies struggle when their sales function remains stuck in outdated methodologies. You've recognized how buyer skepticism, commoditization, and increasing competition demand a fundamental shift in how you approach sales.

The question isn't whether to make this transformation. The question is how to implement it in your specific situation.

This is why I invite you to a focused 90-minute strategy session. In this collaborative diagnostic session, we'll examine exactly how the principles in this book apply to your company. You'll gain clarity about what's really blocking your sales growth and develop a concrete plan for transformation.

By the end of our session, you'll have:

- A clear diagnosis of the specific factors holding back your sales growth

- A deeper understanding of the buyer-first pivot and how it applies to your specific situation

- A detailed implementation plan with timelines and milestones

- A concrete investment roadmap for your transformation

- Answers to all the questions you've formulated while reading this book

Is this session necessary for success? No. Just as some companies successfully implement EOS independently, some will navigate the buyer-first pivot independently. But if you want to accelerate your transformation and avoid common pitfalls, this focused diagnostic session can make the difference between struggle and success.

The market won't wait. Every week that passes with misaligned sales processes and messaging costs you opportunities and reinforces buyer skepticism. Companies that successfully make this pivot will own the future. Those that delay will find themselves increasingly commoditized, competing on price in a race to the bottom.

Book your strategy session using the QR code below. Let's map out your specific path to transformation and ensure your sales function matches the excellence you've built throughout the rest of your EOS implementation.

Scan here for a free consult.

www.ingramcontent.com/pod-product-compliance
Lightning Source LLC
Chambersburg PA
CBHW071712210326
41597CB00017B/2455